SUCCESS IS AUTOMATIC

UNLEASH THE POWER OF YOUR INDUSTRIOUS NATURE AND ACHIEVE YOUR DREAMS

By

Shahid Abdullah
America's Newest Voice on African-American Achievement in the 21st Century

SUCCESS IS AUTOMATIC

Unleash the Power of Your Industrious Nature and Achieve Your Dreams

ISBN - 978-0-578-06469-7

First Edition
Editor: Roz Ayres-Williams
Layout: Mubaashir Uqdah
Cover Design: A.K. Shamsid-Deen
To order, visit www.thegoldentree.com or www.thebilalian.com

My dedication....

With love, deep appreciation and thanks, I dedicate this book to my wife of forty years, Naimah Abdullah. Before passing, she gave her life to rearing four wonderful children and establishing a beautiful family life. Whenever I needed her, she was there with a word or the right action to help me stay on course.

Many family members who loved her miss her dearly. And, because of her work in the community and school system in Roselle, New Jersey, there are hundreds of former students and friends who share in this wonderful memory of a truly beautiful human being.

Thank you.

With love,

Your husband, Shahid

Acknowledgments....

I Thank the Creator for any and all good ideas and thoughts that I am able to pass along to you. My prayer is that these gifts will serve to benefit you.

Thanks to the many researchers and writers, some of whom I have quoted, who studied Success and shared their findings.

I give a special thanks to the late Imam Wallace D. Mohammed for the years of dedication to the restoration of the African-American community and his unique religious insight for the world. It was his thoughts about mankind moving "from Adam's dust to industry" that sparked my interest in writing this book.

I appreciate the work of my close friend and editor, Roz Ayres-Williams, a writer and editorial consultant based in Atlanta, Georgia. She made this endeavor possible.

Thanks also to Barry Pendley, who helped shape the initial look of my book. I thank Mubaashir Uqdah for laying out the pages and A.K. Shamsid-Deen for designing the cover.

I also wish a special thanks to my dear friend, Marcia James Robinson, for her unwavering support, loyalty and vote of confidence. Thanks, Marcia.

Lastly, with thanks and appreciation, I am grateful for the support and encouragement of my children, Jamillah and Rabih. I thank and love them for being there for me.

Preface

The human being was created on the pattern of Human Excellence with an Industrious Nature. This book is about that Industrious Nature and how it operates. Everyone has this nature; it assists us to maneuver automatically in the physical world. It makes our dreams a reality. While we each have different dreams, we have the same Industrious Nature. It is this Nature that makes the human being an Industrious creature. Society has continuously created technology and structures of all kinds; civilization has evolved because of it. This is one aspect that sets the human being apart from the rest of creation.

This innate quality awaits your instructions; you can consciously tap into this power and use it to achieve your dreams. In a step-by-step process, this book will show you how to make your dream a reality.

This book evolved from years of research and practical life experience. I entered the work world with an objective to make a lot of money. After years, sometimes frustrating, of chasing money as my goal, I began to realize that I needed to change my focus.

I began to enthusiastically commit myself to the research and study of what is Success. What I found benefited me tremendously because it forced me to look inside myself at my natural abilities and interests. This introspection led me to pursue my single-most-important-interest fashion design. By releasing and applying my Industrious Nature, I have achieved my dream by designing a new line of shirts and suits for men called **The Bilalian® fashion for men**. This line, with a signature center pocket, represents a new generation in men's fashion that I know will soon take the world by storm.

What I have encountered about myself I now offer to you. My hope is that it will help you soar to your desired level of enjoyment, your own paradise on earth.

While recognizing individual differences, the knowledge I share will maximize anyone's opportunity to succeed. You will find, as I did, that you would not have to look very far for answers because your success is already in you. It is just a matter of knowing how to bring it out.

While reading, you will notice that the word "G-d" is used when referring to the Creator. The problem is that the word "GOD" spells "DOG' in reverse, which is not a good association with the religious concept of the Creator. Imam Wallace D. Mohammed brought this to my attention. He also pointed out that several Jewish organizations were of the same opinion. Therefore, I, too, have adopted the "G-d" spelling.

Shahid Abdullah

For more on Shahid Abdullah's life and personal philosophy, visit his Web site:
www.thegoldentree.com or www.thebilalian.com

SUCCESS IS AUTOMATIC
*Unleash the Power of Your Industrious
Nature and Achieve Your Dreams*

By Shahid Abdullah

"Success is automatic. It is locked in our Nature."

TABLE OF CONTENTS

Ten Steps to Paradise on Earth

Life is not an easy journey, but when you follow the right path, it can be a rich and rewarding one. Below is a basic blueprint for success.

- **Put the Creator first. Start your day with a prayer. Know that He wants you to succeed.**

- **Understand and unleash the power of your Industrious Nature.**

- **Build on the energy that comes from knowing that you were created to be successful.**

- **Trust your senses. Your intuition is a gift from the Creator.**

- **Know that hard work, confidence and sincerity are key components of a winning attitude.**

- **Face all challenges with courage. Fear nothing and have a deep reverence for the Creator.**

- **Respect life, especially human life.**

- Put your money to work for yourself and your community.

- Nourish your mind and body with quality information, food, rest, exercise and recreation.

- Be grateful.

CHAPTER ONE

"Within each of us is the perfect design for Success—a drive created expressly to serve our needs. I call this our Industrious Nature."

-SA

ACKNOWLEDGE YOUR NATURE
The Perfect Design

Your Nature

Most of us like the idea of reaching paradise on earth. It's a worthy, desirable destination that can exist both as a physical reality and a state of mind. However, to paraphrase a popular gospel lyric, "Everybody talking 'bout paradise ain't going there." Whether you end up meandering aimlessly in hell on earth or enjoying the delights of a heavenly condition on earth is entirely up to you. You are the inheritor of the power to shape your destination. Your beliefs, decisions and actions are the major factors that will determine your outcome.

Success is Automatic. It is Locked Within Our Nature.

Within each of us is the perfect design for success—a drive created expressly to serve our needs. Certain aspects of this automatic drive are more easily understood than others. In the physical realm, without any conscious assistance, our hair grows and takes on a natural color, and adult teeth replace baby teeth as we mature. We don't have to do much to help these natural actions along.

Transferring that understanding to a larger view of embedded success becomes more difficult. It takes a while to absorb that we have all the "natural" tools we need to visualize our destination and embark upon a successful course to achieve it. These tools are our Mind, Body, Soul and Will.

The Body—our hardware—was created to carry out the directive of the Mind—our software. The Soul—our program—is the pattern that is designed to guide the innocent nature of the human being. The Will—our power pack—creates a basic desire or drive to successfully meet our needs and fuels the powerful combination of Mind, Body and Soul. These fundamental components form an essence that distinguishes humans from other creatures.

I call this essence our Industrious Nature. When the Will is summoned and channeled through the Mind, Body and Soul, the Industrious Nature automatically locks on a target such as basic survival and goes after it. Our Industrious Nature not only drives us to survive, but also guarantees success in meeting far more ambitious goals for self, family, community and humanity.

Our task is to develop, direct and control our Industrious Nature so that it serves our needs. To determine our quality of life and achieve a chosen goal, we must actively integrate Mind, Body and Soul and apply the right level of Will power to the task. Proper coordination produces the course of action needed to achieve an objective, no matter how minor or lofty. When we coordinate our innate drive, our thinking and our behavior to achieve an end, success is automatically the result.

The Transforming Power of Our Nature

Our way of thinking makes the physical world respond. The Body serves as a tool and a conduit for the Mind. What we feel or think must pass through our physical body to exist in the reality of the world. The Mind, the generator of thought and action, is geared to direct the Body to transform natural matter into man-made products that benefit humankind. This is a natural function of our Industrious Nature.

To our Industrious Nature, dreams and ideas are realities in their premature forms. Most achievements begin as dreams or products of our imagination. The Great Wall in northern China began as a thought. This magnificent wall stands 40 to 50 feet high and measures 15 to 30 feet thick. At one time, it stretched over the countryside of northern China for 3,948 miles—a distance that is twice as long as the state of California. If you started driving in your car at one end of the Great Wall of China today at noon and drove non-stop at 60 miles per hour until noon the next day, you would still have 60 miles to go before you reached the end. Even more amazing than its size is the fact that it was built over 2,000 years ago. A wall that started as a dream in the mind of a Chinese ruler in the Third Century BC ended as one of the Seven Wonders of the World.

Even more remarkable are the recorded achievements in this modern era. According to some scholars, humanity has developed more inventions and ideas in the last 217 years than in our entire history dating back four million years. Airplanes, space flights, cars, computers, oceanic exploration, the list seems endless.

Humanity has accomplished so much in such a short time that we take most of it for granted.

In medicine, for example, doctors now transplant human organs such as the heart and kidney, perform microsurgery on body parts too small for the human eye to see, and alter human responses through chemistry. In technology, scientists and engineers have concentrated energy to create a beam of light so thin that it cannot be seen with the naked eye. Called a laser, this pure concentrated energy is used in medicine to repair delicate organs, arteries and nerves. The computer allows us to compile, organize, store, share and manipulate an enormous amount of information with mathematical precision and at lightening speeds. The Internet has given us access to the world's vast stores of information, interconnecting millions of users in a new age of digital and wireless communication.

All of these innovations are the result of the power of the Industrious Nature to transform the world for our benefit and enjoyment.

Understanding and believing in the power of this natural function takes on special importance for African Americans burdened by a 400-year history that has promoted the concepts of White supremacy and power and Black inferiority and powerlessness.

We must *all* believe—and act upon the belief—that the human being was created with the nature to control, develop and re-shape the physical world. We are not, nor have we ever been, a powerless people. We were—and are today—a transformative people, initiating from our nature new "products" that enhance the quality of life for all mankind. We have transformed music, science and art, sports, medicine and politics, law, language, economics, agriculture, business and so much more. Through our individual and collective Industrial Nature, we, under detrimental social conditions, have rivaled, if not exceeded, the contributions of other cultural or racial groups throughout history. And our work is not done.

CHAPTER TWO

"The use of our Industrial Nature elevates the activities and accomplishments of humans above other creatures."

-SA

UNDERSTAND YOUR NATURE
As a Fully Automatic Function

Understand Your Nature

The Industrious Nature is not some mysterious force working haphazardly in nature. The Creator sealed the Industrious Nature in the anatomy of every single human being in the world. Therefore, you have this quality in you. And no matter who you are or how ambitious your idea or dream, your Industrious Nature is prepared to work for you in the same way it works for other successful people. Human beings need only conceive an idea and the Industrious Nature will begin functioning automatically to make that idea a reality. Unfortunately, too many people stifle the force before it can begin to make a difference.

Fully unleashed, your Industrious Nature will help you overcome tremendous obstacles that may stand in the way of your success. When coupled with a winning attitude—the belief that you will succeed—and the recognition of circumstances that favor success, your Industrious Nature can propel you to greatness.

To make your dreams and aspirations a reality, you must first become aware of the presence of your Industrious Nature. Next, you must gain control of its enormous power for human benefit. Remember, the road to success runs directly from your winning attitude through your Industrious Nature to the real world.

To establish your feet firmly on the platform of success, you should fully understand the origin and existence of the Industrious Nature within you. Its application then becomes an elementary process that puts you on the road to great accomplishments.

Unlike culture and the process of socialization, the Industrious Nature is locked in the structure of the physical body. In essence, the purpose of the physical body is to express the voluntary or involuntary actions of the human being.

All creatures are born with a specific nature and the physical anatomy to manifest it. Birds, for example, are born with wings and all the other appendages including bone structure needed to fly. Fish and other sea creatures are born with everything they need to live in water naturally.

Likewise, we, the most impacting creatures on earth, are born with an Industrious Nature fused with a physical anatomy that enables us to survive—thrive—in our environment. The ability to think, reason, build, move about and communicate is part of our Industrious Nature. The inclination and ability to manifest these actions are not learned behaviors, but inborn. What we *learn* is how to control and direct the behaviors to best serve our needs.

Defining the Industrious Nature

Nature refers to something that occurs automatically (naturally) or needs little or no preparation to develop. It's just the way you are, the way you were naturally created. Eye color is an example of nature. Skin color, hair, teeth and the woman's ability to have children are more examples of nature. These traits are in human beings at birth and, under normal circumstances, will operate or manifest automatically.

Industriousness also is a part of our nature. It is an inborn, innate, inherent characteristic or tendency that exists regardless of social conditions. Scientists, through their extensive studies of the human body, have arrived at a definite opinion about how we function. The brain, feet, ears, mouth, tongue, vocal cords, hands and all the other parts of the body were created for a great purpose, an industrious one – to help human beings obtain their goals and objectives. Our hands, for instance, have four fingers and a thumb. It is the action of the thumb opposed to that of the fingers that makes the hand ideally suited for grasping. Most importantly, these parts of the body operate almost automatically.

In his classic textbook, *Modern Biology*, in which he discusses the human being as the only creature with a truly upright posture, biologist James H. Otto states, "The upright posture freed man's hands so that they could be used entirely for manipulation. Unlike the ape, dog or other creatures, the human being did not have to use his hands to run or achieve balance. We could stand, walk and run perfectly on our two feet." Otto includes other components, stating, "Both of man's eyes see the same vision from slightly different angles, resulting in an improved sense of depth. The combination of intelligence, acute vision, and efficient hands is ideal for the use of tools—an ability peculiar to man."

The power of speech also is possible because of the design of the human body. As a product of the brain, the intellect allows humans to develop their capacity to speak and communicate in many dialects or languages. The tongue, teeth, lips, vocal cords and lungs are all part of the orchestra conducted by the intellect to coordinate sound.

As human beings, we have a rational (ability to think and come to a logical conclusion) component, a moral (sense of right and wrong) component and an emotional (ability to feel) component. These components help us determine *what* to grasp or say and *what* to produce. What goes on in our thinking/feeling/intuitive realm is manifested through our physical body, allowing us to project, through mechanical dexterity, the force of our Industrious Nature. And the use of our Industrial Nature is what elevates the activities and accomplishments of humans above those of other creatures.

Let's look at this concept more closely. The word "industrious," according to the Webster's 20th Century edition, means showing *intelligent* work characterized by *skill* and *cleverness*.

"Intelligent" means that we have the ability to acquire and retain knowledge, to learn from and understand experiences, to respond quickly and successfully to a new situation and to use the faculty of reason to solve problems. Intelligent work is an activity that has or shows a high degree of mental aptitude and ability.

Similarly, the word "clever," as defined by Webster, refers to ingenuity, insight, the ability to learn, devising anything readily and, especially, that which involves or denotes quickness of intellect. Cleverness is a more concentrated area of the intellect.

The word "skillful" means dexterity, aptitude, mastery, ingenuity and wisdom to perform an art, craft, science, judgment or mechanical operation. Essentially, the word skillful means proficiency.

Additionally, "industrious" characterizes earnest, steady hard work—diligence.

We now have the two main components of "industrious," namely, intelligence (characterized by skill and cleverness) and diligence. These components emphasize the need to coordinate intelligence (the Mind) with physical attributes (the Body) to achieve the best results. In other words, we, as human beings, must apply our intelligence along with hard work to get the greatest benefit from our efforts.

CHAPTER THREE

"You were created to be successful as the only intention; failure was never the objective. Instead, guided properly, your nature will rise to fulfill its true objective."

-SA

YIELD TO YOUR NATURE
Through a Winning Attitude

Yield to Your Nature

The Creator has forced you and humanity to move forward in every way imaginable. From the time you were a sperm, He has moved you forward, starting with the journey from your father to your mother. There you moved from among millions of sperm to an egg and became an embryo. Then He forced you to grow into a fetus, and finally into a baby to be born into a strange new world. In fact, your presence in the world is proof that you were created as a winner from the beginning. You should have, therefore, only one attitude—the winning attitude.

In his book, *The Ascent of Man, a Personal View*, a transcript of his 1973 BBC documentary of the same name, Jacob Bronowski says: "Man is a singular creature. He has a set of gifts which make him unique among the animals: so that, unlike them, he is not a figure in the landscape—he is a shaper of the landscape. In body and in mind he is the explorer of nature, the ubiquitous animal, who did not find but made his home in every continent." This indicates that we can use every part of the physical world for our benefit because of our adaptable qualities.

All evidence points to the view that our Industrious Nature functions intuitively and spontaneously. The Industrious Nature was operating within the human being long before humanity understood it or its significance. It was operating as early humans crawled out of the dark womb of ignorance into the light of knowledge and progress. Driven by hunger and the quest to survive, humans drew upon this inherent quality to shape the world around them for their survival and benefit. Then, as now, survival was the driving force that activated the Industrious Nature. And now, as then, success is the outcome for those who apply intelligence, heart and soul to their physical efforts. How high we aim is up to us.

All great achievers have the same basic nature as the rest of us. However, it is the quest for excellence that drives them, the focused fusion of all components of their human nature and their abiding belief that they have all they need to succeed. For them, survival is only the beginning and in some cases a given, but success at building and realizing their own paradise on earth is their goal.

Once you understand the power of your Industrious Nature when combined with a winning attitude, you can draw but one conclusion —success is automatic. You must believe that everything about your physical body is designed for you to enjoy the abundance of life. The human being is born to be successful. It is up to each individual, group, society, civilization or culture to take advantage of these instinctive qualities.

The winning attitude reinforces and directs the power of the Will that is inherent in you to overcome obstacles on your path to success. You are naturally equipped to enhance your evolution by challenging the environment enough to carve out your share of this material world, and responsibly develop your paradise on earth.

When you understand the attributes of the winning attitude, your Industrious Nature, and the evolving process that occurs in creation, you should be convinced that your success and progress are natural outcomes. You were formed to be successful as the only intention; failure is not the objective. Instead, failure is a consequence of misdirected energy. Guided properly, your nature will rise to fulfill its true objective. Success is its only goal.

CHAPTER FOUR

"We must believe and act upon the belief that the human being was created with the intelligence and Will to control, develop and re-shape the physical world."

-SA

ENHANCE YOUR NATURE
Through the Gift of Thinking

Enhance Your Nature

It is our nature to think. Thinking leads to logic, reasoning and wisdom. This forms the basis for success—motivated decision making, whether in lofty arenas such as science or in our everyday lives. Humans invented the wheel and the computer and split the atom because it was in our nature to challenge the creation. Through our senses of touch, smell, taste, hearing and sight, the physical world stimulates our imagination and we begin to think—how can we make this better for self, family, community and all of humankind? Accordingly, the mind challenges and begins to reshape both universes: the internal—how we view and relate to the world—and the external—the physical, social, cultural or other properties of our outer world.

Thinking or rational thought requires the gathering, storing and processing of information (knowledge). Members of each generation are required to follow the progression of rational thought and use what they have learned to improve their condition. Subsequent generations then build upon the gains from the past to benefit the present for the future.

Our success depends on our Will, which, in essence, is the mental power of control over our own actions, physical needs or emotions. The gift of thinking (rational thought) helps us in making a decision — concerning what direction we should take and why—to which the Will would be committed. The Will then disciplines our Mind to focus on our goals and drives us to do what we must to shape our lives accordingly. This function enables us to reach our full potential.

Each of us has Will power, some more of it than others. To put it to good use, we must understand how the Will operates for our benefit and the circumstances that influence it. The phrase, "Mind over matter," is an old but accurate thought, referring to the power of the Will and Mind over the physical or concrete. "Where there is a will, there is a way" also suggests that the Body and various external factors are obedient to the Will and the Mind.

The Will is and does many things:

- It is the force that produces each generation's reality. It harvests and directs the energy of the Industrial Nature to make the physical world comply with our wishes or desires.

- The Will ignites the automatic characteristics of our Industrious Nature and activates the unbeatable optimism of the winning attitude. Most human progress is based on this factor.

- The Will gives the power to overcome odds and can cause people to rise above expectations. Once it is focused on a belief, action or goal, every part of our being must follow suit.

- The Will does not compromise its position and may employ every means possible—even death—to manifest itself and make a way. This is evident even in very young children. Once they decide to do something or refuse to obey the parent, it becomes an impossible task for the adult to restrain them or change their mind without a great deal of struggle and maneuvering. What gives mentally and physically vulnerable children their strength is their Will power.

Hunger strikes are another example of how people apply Will power. The great leader from India, Mohandas (Mahatma) Gandhi, starved himself for more than 40 days because he believed it would help free his people from British rule. A strong human Will does not back down even in the face of death.

If we have any hope of accomplishing our goals, no matter how great, we must activate the powerful force of our Will.

CHAPTER FIVE

"The union of commitment and single-most-important-interest is a winning combination....It will automatically motivate your Industrious Nature to work relentlessly to achieve your goal."

-SA

DIRECT YOUR NATURE
By Focusing on Your Natural Born Interests

Direct Your Nature

It is a fact that people put more energy, intelligence, movement and concentration into those things that interest them most. People accomplish more when they believe in what they are doing. When we have a great interest in what we are trying to achieve, we try harder, work longer and enjoy it more. Matters in which we have little or no interest receive much less attention. Therefore, interest becomes the focus—the key that ignites our Will to its maximum power.

Develop your natural born single-most-important-interest and you will be on the road to fulfilling your dreams and ambitions. Your success is guaranteed because you are likely to be satisfied with yourself when you are doing what you enjoy.

In his book, *Self Motivation,* motivational writer Orison Swett Marden states, "Nothing so strengthens the mind and enlarges the horizon of manhood as a constant effort to measure up to a worthy ambition. It stretches the thought, as it were, to a larger measure, and touches the life to finer issues."

Focusing for success is based on giving your full attention to an idea or endeavor. Energy channeled in one direction will yield the most powerful results. This focused energy breaks through the resistance caused by doubt, indecision and mitigated efforts.

After a 16-year study of the skills needed to achieve peak performance, researcher Charles A. Garfield, Ph.D., concluded that most people who become high achievers committed themselves to a single goal, idea or mission that drove them to perform their best. "Peak performers have a single mission that fires their imagination and to which they are totally committed," he said. Garfield also cited other, lesser factors such as ability, talent or circumstance, but clearly identified commitment to a single mission or interest as the common denominator among high achievers.

Author Stephen R. Covey exemplifies the importance of having a single interest or mission. He advises us in his best-selling book, *Seven Habits of Highly Effective*

People, to begin with the end in mind by developing a personal mission statement or philosophy or creed that "focuses on what you want to be (character) and to do (contributions and achievements) and on the values or principles upon which being and doing are based."

Covey's method highlights the importance of establishing internal controls that will direct your activities regularly toward your goals or interests. When you operate in this manner, your single-most-important-interest governs all the mental and physical activities of your Industrious Nature.

A compelling or singular interest is what motivates people to climb peaks as high as Mount Everest, enter the deepest confines of earth or dive into the dark, seemingly bottomless sea. In fact, not only are people driven to achievement by interest, they may also be willing to take foolish risks to accomplish their goals. This might involve huge personal sacrifices such as loss of life, limb, loved ones or fortunes, and could lead the person to decline, rather than excel, in life.

In some cases, interest may direct our Industrious Nature to *in*activity. If we haven't properly integrated our Mind, Body and Soul or we fail to apply the power of the Will, we might find ourselves always *thinking* about what we want to do—and never actually doing it.

If you're stuck in a rut, remember, no matter who you are, there is very little or no difference between you and highly successful people. You have the same basic make up. You could be on skid row and reading in a discarded magazine about the CEO of a Fortune 500 company. You may feel that you are on the bottom of life, but you have within you the same Industrious Nature as that person. Whatever their goal or achievement—wealth, fame, power, a Nobel Peace Prize—they are not genetically predisposed to achieve more than you. What distinguishes them from you is their choice of endeavor and level of commitment to it. They consciously (or coincidentally) coordinated their Industrious Nature, focused their Will on their single-most-important-interest and found themselves on the path to success.

Your interest, goal and commitment will put you on the path to success and your Will power will keep you fueled for the journey. Once you have selected a goal, task, objective or business based on your single-most-important-interest, you will suddenly experience a driving force that will begin to propel you to heights you once only dreamed were possible. The union of commitment and single-most-important-interest is a winning combination.

Automatically, your Industrious Nature will work relentlessly to achieve your goal. When everything is working in a coordinated fashion, success will come more easily and with a greater enjoyment. The beauty of it all is that you may find that you will accomplish many other objectives while striving for your single-most-important-interest.

Your interest may be stimulated internally (developed in your own mind) or externally (coming from outside of yourself). The important thing is to have one. Without having a clear or defined interest to follow, you can't realize the full benefit of your Industrious Nature; it can't operate to capacity. You will find yourself thinking that your life is incomplete or has no meaning and that you are ineffective. However, once you establish your interest, especially your single-most-important-interest, and it becomes your mission, your Industrious Nature will automatically move to give your life back its purpose.

Steps to Finding Your Purpose

Your purpose is your personal gold mine. All you have to do is find it. You must firmly believe that you were created for a good purpose and that your success is inevitable. Then let the power of your Mind and Soul take flight to create your vision of paradise on earth.

Discovering your single-most-important-interest is the key to knowing your purpose in life. Once you know your interest or purpose, commit your energy to it. The minute you apply the power of your Will, your desire to succeed will begin to manifest physically. You automatically will begin to develop your goals, ideas and concepts, seek the help you need, and find the resources and opportunities that will lead you closer to your goals.

Use this simple "goal and interest selection formula" to determine what turns you on. It doesn't make any difference whether your interest is helping illiterate adults learn to read, starting your own business or becoming a better parent. The basic steps to success are the same.

1. Begin by making a list of all your interests. Do not leave out anything. List all the ideas, concepts and endeavors you find interesting. The list can be as long or short as you like.

2. Select no more than three of the interests you find most compelling and establish a personal goal for each one. For example, if singing is a personal interest, decide what you'd like to do with your talent—develop it through lessons, audition for American Idol, join the state mass choir, make a jazz demo, become a Broadway star, etc.

3. Set a time limit (e.g., 30 days) to examine your list. Study each interest/goal and note the pros and cons of pursuing each. Imagine the benefits and how you would feel (emotionally) if you accomplished each of the goals. Think of the financial or emotional rewards (if any) of each. Consider your position in life and visualize how it would change when you reach each particular goal.

4. Give yourself at least 30 more days to consider what it would take to do each of the three. For example, one goal may require that you get more education or formal training. If your goal is to start a business, you may need to connect with your local Small Business Development Center for information on preparing a business plan or finding start-up funds.

5. Next, do a serious comparison of each of your three goals or interests. Ask yourself, if you could achieve only one, which one would it be? Which seems the most compelling and practical? Listen to both your intuition and your rational mind when making your choice.

6. When you are ready, take the major step of selecting the goal or interest that means the most to you. You must trust your instincts. Once you have arrived at your single-most-important-interest or mission, give it your undivided attention. Stand by it firmly!

7. List all the steps you must take each day or week to advance your goal – then apply your Will to the

task of completing each step. It won't always be easy, but you will find the tasks more enjoyable than those associated with a more casual interest or goal.

Always trust in the Creator and your good senses. The more you trust yourself or your judgment, the more energy and commitment you will put into your idea, dream or objective.

When you turn your whole self (your Industrious Nature) to your interest, you will find yourself on the road to success. Be confident in the fact that you are the leader of your destiny!

CHAPTER SIX

"Commitment, devotion and
mental toughness are best
developed through the practice
of self-restraint.**"**

-SA

CONTROL YOUR NATURE
Through Self-Mastery

Control Your Nature

The ultimate goal of adults is to control their own destiny. Before we can chart our own course in the sea of life, we must first establish control of ourselves. No success comes into existence without certain conditions. Ideas, actions and circumstances within our environment can influence our own thoughts and conduct. The only way we control these influences is by taking charge of our lives. How purposefully we develop and control our inner thoughts, feelings and actions determines our success in life.

At the core of all success is self-mastery. This principle is inherent in the disposition of success. Self-mastery is the link to all progress and forms a pattern for the design of creation.

Self-mastery will keep you focused and on course. The discipline within you will help you to carry out the steps that are needed for achievement. Conditioning your mind for success and developing the skills and knowledge to reach your goals also contribute to your overall salvation and growth as a human being.

Belief in yourself and your Creator is your starting point. You must believe that you are unique, created to be of value to yourself and society. You must believe that your true self is connected to the essence of creation and the Creator. You are not a mistake or accident, but part of the Creator's plan. Your existence is intentional or at the very least, a won presence. You must begin everything with the winning attitude and believe that you were born to be successful. Trust your choices, decisions and most of all the talents and abilities given to you by G-d.

The areas that must be honed to achieve self-mastery are your use of imagination, work ethic, continued education, capacity for self-restraint, ability to share, and sense of oneness with the creation. Within each area, you must develop certain attitudes and habits that will facilitate the work of your Industrious Nature.

Habits, which are ways of thinking and acting until the methods become automatic, are the most vital and elemental factors of success. The ultimate goal would be to develop all good behavior into habits. Author Stephen R. Covey, in his book, *Seven Habits of Highly Effective People,* defines the habits in this way: "Because they are based on principles, they bring the maximum long-term beneficial results possible. They become the basis of a person's character, creating an empowering center of correct maps from which an individual can effectively solve problems, maximize opportunities, and continually learn and integrate other principles in an upward spiral of growth."

Although there are many good habits, three that can most quickly clear your path to success are use of your imagination, having a good work ethic, and the investment of time and money in the continuation of your education.

Another three that are important contributors to the quality and enjoyment of your success are developing self-restraint, sharing with others, and being one with humanity. Many people who manage to make an impact on the world lack these three habits. Often they become achievers who feel unappreciated or out of touch with others. They may turn their personal vision of paradise on earth into a living hell for others, or never feel satisfied, joyful or grateful when they reach their goals.

When you establish a balanced range of positive attitudes and habits as part of your daily life, you will find that success is, indeed, automatic, and that you will fully enjoy the blessings of your paradise on earth.

Let's look more closely at each of these habits.

Use of the Imagination

There are some things you can do without and still be successful, but the imagination is not one of them. The imagination is the seat of human creativity. All that humankind has created sprang directly from the imagination. Our vision for the future resides there as well. This mental tool is a powerful and priceless asset to your development and progress.

Everyone has the power to imagine. With practice, you can learn to clearly visualize your ideas, plans, goals and, most importantly, their completion. You can *see* your success and actually *visualize* yourself achieving it. Dr. Charles Garfield, a leading authority on high performance, calls this "mental rehearsal."

"Mental rehearsal, the process of imprinting mental images of successful actions in the mind's eye, is used by peak performers to practice mental positive outcomes and achievements that they ultimately do attain in reality," he explains.

In his *Peak Performance* program, Dr. Garfield describes the use of the imagination in this manner as a "master skill" that peak performers use to guard against the stagnation of idleness and to improve upon or develop new skills.

"Mental rehearsal is far from casual daydreaming. It requires concentrated and repeated practice," Dr. Garfield states. "In mental rehearsal, clarity of the image is of utmost importance. Whether your goal relates to a personal relationship, artistic activity, business dealing, athletic contest or any other endeavor, the image must be sharp and clear. And it must depict extraordinary performance."

In conclusion, Dr. Garfield writes, "Also essential to successful mental rehearsal is control. Control is the manipulation of the image to the extent that the image becomes, to the mind, reality. You might first watch yourself achieve your goal, as if you were only an observer. Then remove yourself from the observer's role, and imagine yourself, in complete detail, actually achieving the objective."

Clearly, it pays to develop the powerful and valuable skill of mental rehearsal into a habit.

No matter how old or young, or rich or poor you are, your imagination is the power that can propel you to success. Not only is it important that you believe in your success, but you also must see yourself as successful and achieving. Think about it regularly and meaningfully.

- Establish mental rehearsal as a daily routine in your life. Each morning before you start your day, rehearse in your mind's eye your goals and plans, the ones you are working on and the future ones. You should outline your actions for that day and see yourself achieving each objective. Allow yourself to feel what it is like to complete your plan.

- To begin this practice, set your alarm clock 15 to 30 minutes earlier than usual. This early start will give you that extra time each morning to establish this process. Rise and, in the manner in which you are accustomed and with absolute concentration, pray to your Lord and Creator. After prayer, focus your energy by inhaling and exhaling slowly and deeply eight to 12 times. After you vitalize your Mind and Soul, quietly direct your mental energy to visualize your daily activities. Focus on your goals and tasks for the day and see yourself achieving them. This mental rehearsal will help you to commit yourself—and your Will—to action.

The imagination is the fuse that sparks new and great ideas. Through the imagination, humans learned to fly, develop computers, create jazz, transplant human organs and walk on the moon. You might not be aware of the next great ideas that are residing in the human mind, but they are there. All you have to do is act on the blessed and glorious power of your imagination— and *you* may bring the next great idea to light!

Don't be afraid to have big dreams and never short-change yourself by killing your dream or dreaming too little. People with big dreams, and who act upon them, often end up producing new realities for the world. Let your imagination soar. You are only limited by your expectations.

Having a Good Work Ethic

Establish consistent and regular work hours and sensible priorities. While your family always comes first, you (and they) must learn to respect your work schedule. Develop a sense of the value of time and how to use it in a balanced way. There are only 24 hours in a day. You will spend six to eight hours resting or sleeping. You must take time for eating, relaxation and family. Therefore, how effectively you use the time you have left becomes crucial. Devote it to your goal, mission or idea. Try not to let friends, irrelevant situations or nonessential activities take your time away from this work. Once you establish your work schedule, stick to it. Learn to build your other activities around it.

1. Automate and simplify your work. Learn to use a computer to help stay organized and make the best

use of your time. Track your tasks and appointments, follow up with key contacts, pay your bills, shop, stay in touch with family and friends, search for information, stay abreast of current events, and follow up on important opportunities using the computer. You will find that simplifying your life through mastery and application of technology will help clear the path to success.

2. As a general rule, don't put off until tomorrow what you can do today because this practice only doubles or triples your load. When you don't keep up, it's harder to catch up. Remember, procrastination is death to progress. Stay organized. Focus on what is most important. Keep written records of tasks to be done and of those that have been done. Follow a written schedule of daily activities. This prepares you for the decision-making process.

3. Leave nothing to chance. First, develop a broad overview of your entire plan for success. The plan should consist of goals, objectives and tactics. Your goal is your end point, the objectives are the measurable targets you must hit along the way to

reach the goal, and the tactics are the actions you will take to achieve your objectives and, ultimately, the goal. You are, in a sense, creating a business plan for your life. Your plan provides a framework that will give momentum to your goals.

4. Chart your activities on an hour-to-hour, day-to-day, week-to-week and monthly basis. Major goals are accomplished by completing the sustaining goals one at a time.

5. Don't be afraid to make decisions. Base your decisions on information, your motives or purpose and the desired outcome (goal). Think clearly and trust your intuition. Don't be afraid of making a mistake. That type of fear will prevent you from making any decision, good or bad. Failure to decide or act almost always translates into a loss. You can move forward with a wrong decision better than with no decision. When you make a mistake, you have an opportunity to correct it for the sake of progress and grow from it. You also will be less likely to make the same mistake again. This will put you farther ahead and help you become a better decision maker.

Summing up the work ethic, Grant G. Gard in his book, *Championship Selling*, explains the importance of being thorough. He stated, "Go at every activity without giving thought to the possibility of defeat. Concentrate on your strengths and not on your weaknesses. Be determined to follow through on every point in your goal achievement plan."

Commitment to Your Education

With the future on your doorstep and technology already sitting in your living room, you must devote a portion of your time and earnings to keeping up with the times. Life is a continuous process and learning is a vital part of it. While it is your responsibility, absolutely, solely and without reservation, to ensure that your children are properly educated, it's just as important to continue your own education, whether formally or informally.

Education, a natural process in human development, becomes a lifeline to your future progress and prosperity. When you stop learning, life becomes dull, regression stunts your growth, and progress comes to a screeching halt.

If you didn't finish high school, take steps to obtain a G.E.D. If you dropped out of college, it's never too late to go back and get your degree in the field that interests you most and will best support your plans for success. If you need to upgrade your skills for a better paying job, attend a technology school. Get your master's degree, if that is your dream. Go for the doctorate if that will take you closer to your paradise on earth.

Education doesn't come only from a school or college. It is available informally through videos, books and magazines, the Internet, online courses, documentaries, community seminars and the shared experiences of other people. There are countless sources of knowledge.

Fortunately, your Industrious Nature fights for your education, no matter how old you are. You may try to shut yourself off from information, but it is virtually impossible. From head to toe, your body is a receiver for information. Your senses of touch, sight, sound, taste and smell are designed to take in information at a much faster and more precise rate than you can express outwardly. In fact, in this era of "information overload," your task is to cut through the clutter and focus on absorbing only that which adds value to your lifestyle, mission and purpose in life.

You must embrace and internalize the self-education habit. Learn about what you would like to do and how to do it. Then, continue to improve upon your understanding and competency. There are do-it-yourself books, manuals and videos, and all types of computer programs that teach you new activities, help you brush up on skills or advance you to new levels of competency.

You can learn how to start, maintain and expand a business, speak a foreign language, create a Web site, paint your house, write a book, organize a community drive, build a better relationship with your children or parents, improve your health, grow plants, whatever will enrich your life and move you closer to achieving your vision of paradise on earth. Never lose your curiosity about the world around you.

Practicing Restraint

Anyone who's tried to lose 20 pounds knows that self-mastery is easier said than done. But it's a worthy and necessary pursuit. Although self-mastery begins with belief and is maintained by positive habits, it is strengthened through the practice of restraint. Learning to control your emotions, indulgences, obsessions, compulsions and passions can deepen your enjoyment of life and success. It can help you balance your priorities and sharpen your senses.

Many of us are most challenged in the area of healthy living—which enriches the Mind, Body and Soul and is vital to our success. We've already discussed what will fuel your Mind and Soul. But your Body also needs special attention. In fact, this area often requires the biggest application of self-restraint. Too many of us battle food, drug and alcohol addictions that damage our health and chances for happiness.

The Body thrives on energy, regularity and balance and must be revitalized each day, through adequate sleep, proper diet and exercise, so that it can manifest the desires of your Industrious Nature. Eat a balanced diet of fresh, enzyme-rich fruits, meats and vegetables, drink naturally soothing and energizing teas and fresh water. Stretch your body each morning and absorb the energy of nature through deep breathing, outdoor walks and meditation. Keep regular hours and allow your body to wake itself naturally at the same time each day. Pay attention to warning signs, see a doctor regularly or when necessary, and avoid ingesting poisons such as cigarette smoke, excessive fats and sugars, non-prescribed drugs and excessive amounts of alcohol. And don't forget to practice safety habits such as wearing a seat belt when driving.

People with food addictions are often called "emotional eaters." They are asked to deal with their emotional problems before embarking on a weight loss program. This battle with our feelings underlies one of the most serious challenges to self-mastery—emotionalism.

Controlling Emotionalism

Our emotional makeup confuses us more than anything else in our nature. Our emotions tend to accept what feels good and reject whatever feels bad. As a consequence, emotions can lead us into something bad because it initially feels good, or they can lead us away from something that is beneficial to us because it initially feels uncomfortable or annoying. Emotions not under the control of intellect or morality can lure you far from the path of success and cause you to lose everything that you have built for yourself and those you love. Scores of great people, organizations, nations and ideas have crumbled under the deceptive and detrimental direction of emotion.

Left unguarded, emotionalism has a tendency to dominate everything, to manipulate and control us. We must balance our emotional side with our intellectual and moral components. When balanced, our emotions become appropriate to the situation. We would not laugh at someone else's misfortune or feel joy when they are sad. However, when our emotions are allowed to rule over the other components, we may fail to exercise discretion and balanced judgment.

Feelings don't generate themselves; they come into existence only after an action. They have no principles, rationality, moral commitment or perception of wrong or right. They are just reactions. They can be your best friend or your worst enemy. If they are in a balanced and cooperative position with your rational and moral self, they are wonderful. But if the emotions are in control of you, success that reflects positive human qualities will be out of your reach. When the emotions are controlled, one can make decisions with a morally inspired, more rational mind.

As with the body, we must pay attention to emotional warning signs. We know from experience that what feels good *to* us is not necessarily good *for* us. We know that, while enchantment or a sense of euphoria is a pleasurable feeling, what we do to achieve that feeling sometimes comes at a dear price to our mental, spiritual and physical well-being.

Restraint is our best defense against the power of emotionalism. Emotional restraint prevents your thoughts from becoming clouded with greed, envy, jealousy, prejudice and any other negative feelings that will block your progress, or your understanding of humanity and its progress.

Everything we attempt in life should be led by our moral self and informed by our intellect, with emotions supplying the enthusiasm we need to be successful. Properly integrated, emotions will energize our desire to achieve, motivate us to transcend obstacles and give us pleasure in our accomplishments. However, left unchecked, emotions will utterly consume and ruin our entire life and the lives of others.

Battling Abuse

Every vice or destructive addiction known to man enters through the emotional self. In this sense, the emotions can be a gateway to hell on earth.

Substance abuse (alcohol, nicotine, cocaine, heroin or any other narcotic) would quickly lose its appeal if these substances had to enter the body through our intellectual or moral components. As scrutinizers, our intellectual and moral selves would condemn these substances as detrimental to the Industrious Nature. The intellect would weigh the destructive powers of drugs on the human Mind, Soul and Body and reject them. Understanding what addiction does to the family, the community and our overall quality of life, our moral self would urge us to drive dangerous substances from the community. But the emotions, not the intellect or morality, are the portal for substance abuse. Your imbalanced emotional state will direct your body to accept the substance. Once your brain is seduced by the substance to generate a feeling of euphoria, you enter the realm of pure feeling, experiencing an artificial sense of joy or peace—an emotional high. The substance dulls the senses and causes you to develop a false sense of security.

This artificial high lasts only as long as the substance is in the body. As your feelings begin to drift downward from the high, you are already "thinking" about what it will take to get back to where you were. Eventually, as your senses become more deadened, you find yourself having to take a little more of the substance or take it more frequently to avoid the ever spiraling "downs" that suddenly make life unbearable.

Having signaled that you have a goal, your Will then fuels your drive to go to any lengths to satisfy the craving now manifested by the Body. The Industrial Nature is thus activated by emotions that find no counterbalance in rational thought, soaring spirit or culturally grounded soul.

The damage that this dependency does to human life is visible, scattered throughout the streets, alleys, homes, families, jails and hospitals of America and the world.

Substance abusers in most cases need clinical help to break the chains of addiction. But they also have within them the same tools for a successful outcome as anyone else. While they are receiving treatment, they can support themselves by directing every ounce of their energy and Will to the practice of self-restraint.

Clearly, self-restraint is easier for some people than others. But, when you use goal setting, engage in mental rehearsals to visualize yourself achieving your goal, and apply the full power of your Will, your Industrious Nature will start to make the right things happen for you.

Breaking Away

Test your powers. Decide to stop doing something that you were previously unable to give up. People with an exceptionally strong will have been known to stop a bad habit or addiction cold turkey. Others need a more gradual approach, such as the one outlined below. Whether your goal is to stop smoking, give up alcohol or pills or lose weight, this formula can work for you:

The first week, focus on abstaining from the use of the adverse substance or the over-indulging habit for only one day.

The second week, abstain for two consecutive days.

The third week, abstain for three consecutive days.

Finally, abstain for the entire week.

Repeat the process, substituting weeks for days and months for weeks.

With the possible exception of emotional overeaters struggling to lose weight, the main emphasis should be on the task and not the problem. Most importantly, once you have completed your abstinence program, the substance or habit no longer will have power over your emotions or mind and your dependency will be diminished or completely gone. Once you are in full control of your Mind and Body, your Industrious Nature will function to your benefit and not to your detriment. Your task from that point on is to practice emotional restraint and ensure that your rational self and moral self are the masters of your emotions.

The step-by-step formula can also be applied in an affirmative way to build good habits and complete tasks. Instead of abstaining from something, make yourself do something you normally don't do. Use the formula to develop new skills, participate in a particular activity, meet with people to complete a project, or practice a healthy habit.

It should now be clear that restraint is the key to controlling the emotions. Restraint is an indispensable tool for shaping a better you through self-discipline, the core of self-mastery. If you fall off track, don't beat yourself up. Take a deep breath and get back into the game.

Practicing Self-Restraint Through Fasting

The most effective way to balance, tone and coordinate your Mind, Soul, Body and Will is through the practice of self-restraint. We develop self-restraint through sacrifice—the act of abstaining from something you desire or (think you) need.

The enforced absence of something you desire helps to cleanse the Mind, Soul and Body of impurities, focus energy, emotions and thoughts and build resistance to negativity and temptation. Through self denial, you will emerge a more disciplined, focused person. Denying yourself something you don't really care about having is cheating. Temptation must exist in order for the Will to prove its mettle in the battle against desire. You can't be tempted when there is no desire.

People have difficulty discerning between what they need and what they want. Through sacrifice, you may discover that a lot of what you always thought you needed is actually only a want. Not only will you gain respect for the power of the Will, but you will begin to have a mental picture of success uncluttered by useless "things" and more focused on progressive values and contributions to society. Sacrifice is character building.

The most common form of self-restraint is fasting. People fast for many reasons—to observe religious holidays, lose weight, cleanse the body, fight sickness or break a bad habit. Fasting does not necessarily mean living on bread and water for a prescribed length of time. The length of time you fast can vary. What your fast consists of can vary. It can be a brief self-regulated fast (for short periods of up to three days) or a long-range fast under the direction of a medical professional. It can be a partial fast that lasts until sundown or consists of your eating only certain foods and avoiding others.

The one thing you should never deprive your body of is water. Be sure to drink it during any fasting period lasting longer than eight hours. Also be sure to check with your doctor or medical advisor before beginning any fasting program that will last longer than a day or two or that will drastically alter your food intake. When done properly, fasting cleanses your body. This strengthens the Spirit, and it compels the Mind to focus. It allows enzymes normally used for digesting food to concentrate on healing damaged tissue and other problems, and helps build self-discipline and character.

The best fasts are those found in religious teachings. Al-Islam, Christianity and Judaism teach fasting from their religious scriptures. In Al-Islam, believing men and women are expected to fast (abstain from food, drink and sex) during the daylight hours at least once each year for the entire month of Ramadan. This is a prescribed fast. Similarly, Christians fast during the Lenten Season to commemorate the 40 days Christ spent praying and fasting in the wilderness. The Jewish people have been practicing the principles of fasting for thousands of years. It is also recorded that for thousands of years Buddhists and Native Americans have fasted regularly as a way of life.

Whatever your motivation, you should practice the fasting with a conscience determination to complete the task. Give your Will a chance to do its work.

Looking deeply into the value of self-restraint, you will observe that self-denial gives rise to a strong sense of devotion within you. The tougher the denial challenge becomes, the more devoted or committed you become to the cause of overcoming it. This amplifies into a larger sense of commitment to any cause or idea that is important to you.

Commitment and devotion are absolutely necessary in attaining or sustaining success. You must have the mental toughness to overcome obstacles and press forward after falling short of your desired goal. These traits, commitment, devotion and mental toughness, are best developed through the practice of self-restraint.

The Ability to Share

Perhaps the easiest feature to overlook in your quest for achievement is the value of sharing or giving back to the community or society. We may be able to visualize our own growth and success, but not see any reason to share ourselves with others as part of that growth.

Of course, any practical business owner, athlete, entertainer or other achiever knows that he must make some effort to honor the community that forms his or her customer base or audience. But is the achiever's attitude that one only has to give enough back to attract sales or fans? Or does he believe that his customers or fans have contributed to his success and therefore deserve all that he can afford to share with them?

While some people believe that giving back to their community is essential for their own continued growth, far too many achievers veer away from sharing. Did you know that African Americans give proportionately less back to their own communities than any other racial or ethnic group in America? In too many instances, we invest our talent, intelligence and wealth outside of our communities and nourish cultures other than our own.

For many of us, achieving means acquiring money, power and knowledge—and there is certainly nothing wrong with that. But no one achieves within a vacuum. Your success is not alienated from society; it is communal. There are always people along the way who have helped you, institutions that have taught or supported you, economic, historical, cultural and social circumstances that have shaped you, and giants who have inspired you. They form a community of support. And that community deserves to receive a portion of your time, knowledge, experience and wealth as repayment. This is how a community is sustained as a continuing source of inspiration and support for others.

The true value of your success is measured by what you do or have done for society, starting with the one closest to home—the culture or community that gave birth to you. Consider it a mutual exchange. If your growth is the result of what you received from society, then it stands to reason that society's growth is the result of what it receives from you.

When the wealthy or talented do not give to the society in proportion to what they gain or receive from society, serious problems arise. We see this principle at work here in the Americas, in Africa and many of the Eastern European countries.

The haves are responsible for maintaining a tenable balance among all elements of their society. When those who have achieved continue to take from those who have not yet achieved and don't give back proportionally, the balance is upset and the culture or society begins to crumble. The achievers become corrupt and the masses become vengeful. This situation leads to unrest, rebellion and ultimately war. Interestingly, what often when a war or calamity ends, and the dust settles, those at the top start to lose their grip on power and those at the bottom begin to emerge as the new achievers.

But we don't need a world history lesson to illustrate the importance of sharing to sustain balance and growth. Do one good thing for your community and sit back and enjoy the good feelings that will emanate from your Soul. The more you do or give, the better it feels. Do yourself a favor and make it a habit to reinvest at least five to 20 percent of your time, talent or treasure in your community.

You will have the added pleasure of serving as a role model and influence in the lives of young people. A community in which everyone, from the wealthiest to the poorest, works together to benefit its members; particularly its children, is a vital and successful community. Also, children who see you participating in the community will strive to emulate your success.

Those who have not yet achieved need to know it is possible. Your example may be all they need to gain the necessary confidence. Even if you are just at the point of setting your goals and aspiring to achieve them, make service—sharing—a habit. Start by spending a part of each week helping someone who needs a hand up.

Achieving Oneness Through Unity

Sharing helps you in another very important sense. It increases your sense of oneness with Humanity. The linking of Mind, Body and Humanity is essential to the over-all picture for human productivity. A small mind can think only of itself. A great mind can think of itself and others on a universal plane and considers itself an essential part of life's grand plan.

Think of how your body operates. Each part of your body functions independently as well as together for the good of the whole. You must see yourself operating within Humanity in the same manner. Each person functions independently as well as with others for the good of the whole—the progress of Humanity.

The progress of Humanity and your progress are linked as a chain in the eternal splendor of time—past, present and future. When you move forward, Humanity moves forward. When Humanity leaps into the future, it carries you with it.

Unity symbolizes power. It does not mean "the same as" or "uniformity." It does not refer to a collective that suppresses the individuality of people. Rather, it is the act of individuals coming together—the principle that brings about change in a society. This form of unity liberates the individual, whose capacity to contribute to the whole is restricted only by his or her commitment, ability and understanding.

Most leaders invoke unity when seeking change, influence or control. Their goal is to get more people to commit to the same goal. This produces a unified body. Without it, leaders have no power.

Humanity's greatest progress occurs when individuals pool their resources and work together. As social creatures, unity is a natural direction for humans to choose. Progress is the nature of humanity, and the liberation of the individual (the growth of self) only accelerates that process. Part of this liberation resides in our differences. Therefore, we must respect our differences and learn from them. Another part lies in our sameness, which forms common ground based on interests, abilities and goals.

CHAPTER SEVEN

"You are created to be useful to yourself and others."

-SA

CULTIVATE YOUR NATURE
And Benefit Humanity

Success and the Individual

"Like crabs in a barrel," is an old concept most of us have heard about since we were very young. While it can refer to any group, it was used in respect to the African-American community during the 50's, perhaps even earlier.

The crabs would never let one of the group escape the barrel. Every time one crawled high enough to the top to get out, one of the others would reach up and pull it back down.

The crab-in-the-barrel behavior exists in the African-American community today. Fueled by jealousy, envy and self abasement, this attitude continues to consume our community to the point that we do not help or want to see each other progress. As in nature, this attitude prevents group progress which is essential to the sound growth and success of the individuals within the group.

Success begins with the individual and ends with the society. As you develop your single-most-important-interest, you will begin to visualize concepts and ideas. This is an automatic function. The mind opens to the universe and what the material world has to offer. The intellectual properties of the mind turn the physical world inside out until the light of understanding comes on. At this point, you will realize that the universe was created to challenge you to get the best use out of it and yourself.

Ideas never come to the group or society simultaneously. It does not make any difference how grand or menial the ideas are, they come to the individual and spread to the public. In some cases, more than one individual may get the same or a similar idea. Likewise, from time to time, inventions such as the airplane are passed from one generation to the next before they become a reality. However, it is the individual who is the conduit that brings the concepts into the society. The individual gets an idea, works on it and when it becomes too much to handle alone, he or she seeks the assistance of others to develop the concept. When that happens, the person is on the threshold of creating an industry.

An excellent example of this process is the light bulb, invented by Thomas Edison. On January 19, 1883, Edison created the world's first standardized incandescent electric lighting system employing overhead wires. His trial run took place in Roselle, a small town in New Jersey. This experiment proved to be an idea that lit up the world.

Today, homes and buildings all over the world are able to function at night as well as day because of Edison's efforts. From power plants to appliances used in nearly every home, industries sprang from his concepts.

Edison is just one example of an individual making a contribution to humanity. Many others are not as well known, but they still have had a tremendous impact on our lives.

Imagine, it takes hundreds of industries and thousands of people to manufacture the products you use everyday. More important, everything in your material world was developed from the ideas introduced by an individual. The value of the individual is immeasurable.

The Connection

It is not a coincidence that the words "individual" and "industry" appear to be connected. A closer analysis reveals an absolute interdependence, with smaller words within them defining their dependency.

"Individual" is composed of three words (*in, divide* and *dual*). The *in* expresses inclusion. *Divide* means to separate into equal parts by a divisor. This indicates that the part is equal to or has the same ingredients as the whole. *Dual* implies having two or double the parts. Fundamentally, individual means the end result of something that has been separated into the smallest common denomination. Simply put, in the absence of all of humanity except one person, that one person represents humanity.

"Industry" comprises four smaller words (*in, dust* and *try*). *Dust* means powdery earth or other matter in bits fine enough to be easily suspended in air. It also refers to a humble or spiritless condition, or anything worthless, illustrating the powerful concept of "from dust to industry." As with the word individual, *in* expresses inclusion, but it also means "within," which is the closer meaning in this instance. It refers to what is made out of the dust that is most important. *Try* is the simple, direct word for putting forth the effort to do something even in the face of difficulties. It suggests a striving to overcome obstacles or to free oneself from an impediment. (An example is a person who struggles to be the best runner even though he or she was born with a heart problem.)

In other words, the human being began as a humble creation. Then, as a species, through a period of trial and effort, the human grew to develop the social, economic and scientific components that create societies that are supported by industry.

In essence, both words, individual and industry, identify the human being as having an Industrious Nature. Each individual has a particular part in exploring that nature. As an individual, you must give a great deal of attention to your ideas or concepts, and treat them as if they are gold. They can be the genesis of the next industry that benefits humanity.

CHAPTER EIGHT

"You are created to achieve your goals and share in the wealth. You can accomplish this by improving on yourself one day at a time and achieving one goal at a time. Each success will build on itself as you reach for the stars."

-SA

APPLY YOUR NATURE
And Enjoy Automatic Success

Apply Your Nature

Life expects you to succeed, and you have the basic tools to do so. Your Industrious Nature operates automatically to turn your purpose into a reality through which the dreams, ideas and aspirations of humanity may flow and flourish. You have within you the natural ability to envision, create and enjoy your own paradise on earth. All you have to do is add the winning attitude and self-mastery to the mix.

The Time to Begin is Now

You *must* make your mark in this life. There is a share of this world that belongs to you—and there is no better time to start laying claim to it. The circumstances are right—not yesterday, not next year, but right now. Don't be like the person who travels around the world and misses all the beautiful sights, sounds and unique activities along the way. Open your heart, mind and eyes to life and take the opportunity to partake of all this world has to offer. Know without a doubt that you are created to achieve your goals and share in the world's wealth.

Remember, there is a direct connection and relationship between you and society. Every part of your body and mind was created for your own personal success as a prerequisite for human progress. Therefore, your worthiness is determined by how useful you are to yourself, your family and your community.

CHAPTER NINE

"Your Industrious Nature will obey your Will regardless of your age, race, sex, economic status or beginning in life."

-SA

UNLEASH YOUR POWER
Achievers and Their Industrious Nature

With this power, you can—and will—achieve your dreams just as so many before you. The pages of history are filled with the lives of achievers who followed their single-most-important-interest to a wonderful result. Some of them began life very meekly and were unbelievably poor, while others were born with the so-called silver spoon in their mouth. Regardless of their beginnings, these achievers shared one thing in common: they followed their single-most-important-interest and allowed their Industrious Nature to propel them to success.

One the best examples of this is a woman who began her life as Anna Mary Robertson on September 7, 1860. By the time she died 101 years later, she had raised five children and accomplished what you read about in story books. Born in Greenwich, New York, Robertson left home at the age of twelve to work as a "hired girl" on a neighboring farm. At age twenty-seven, she married Thomas Salmon Moses and moved to the Shenandoah Valley in Virginia. After eight years in Virginia, she returned to New York State with her husband and five surviving children.

After forty-three years, her husband passed, leaving her to face a future shaped by her own hands.

Mary Moses turned her attention to her single-most-important-interest, the visual arts in fine embroidery. She embroidered pictures for friends and family until she contracted a serious case of arthritis that prevented her from using her hands for such fine needle work.

Now in her seventies, and seemingly cut off from her love of the arts, Moses searched for another avenue to express her interest, one that required less finger dexterity.

Driven by her Industrious Nature, she purchased an oil painting kit complete with brushes, oil paints, and a small canvas. Thus began the career of one of the most famous American painters in history. With no formal training, completely self-taught, Moses began painting distinctively beautiful pictures of folksy rural landscapes.

According to Wikipedia, an online encyclopedia, her work soon came to the attention of collectors all over the world, and her paintings became highly sought after, particularly in Europe and Japan. In 1940, she had the first ever one-woman exhibition in New York and a special presentation at Gimbel's department store. By now, she had acquired the nickname of "Grandma Moses."

Grandma Moses generated more than 3,600 canvasses over three decades, satisfying a demand that never diminished during her lifetime. She became so well known that Hallmark used her rural scenes for their greeting cards. As late as 2006, one of her works, *Sugaring Off*, which was a prime example of her signature folk art style, sold for $1.2 million. Another of her paintings, *Fourth of July*, honoring President Eisenhower, still hangs in the White House.

As described by many historians and writers, Grandma Moses is one of the most important self-taught artists of the 20th century, and was arguably the first artist to become a media superstar. In 1949, President Harry S. Truman presented her with the Women's National Press Club Trophy Award for outstanding accomplishment in art. In 1951, she appeared on *See It Now*, a television program hosted by Edward R. Murrow. In 1960, New York Governor Nelson Rockefeller proclaimed the occasion of her 100th birthday "Grandma Moses Day" in her honor. Her unique style and influence may be seen in art and illustration to this day.

What is so remarkable about Grandma Moses is the fact that she officially began her painting career when she was about 78 years old, showing that the proof of the pudding is in the taste. If you think that you are too old to get started with your dream, remember, it is all in your mind. Grandma Moses proved that you are never too old to start to live your dream.

Your Industrious Nature never grows old or stops working: it will function until your body "turns to dust." It does not have an expiration date.

The power of the Industrious Nature exemplified in Grandma Moses is in every human being. It is just a matter of letting it flow freely without inhibitions. Howard Schultz is another example of a successful achiever who followed his concept or brainchild to fulfill his dream.

This noted American businessman and entrepreneur is best known as the chairman and CEO of Starbucks and a former owner of the Seattle SuperSonics.

In 2006, *Forbes Magazine* ranked Schultz as the 354th richest person in the United States, with a net worth of $1.1 billion dollars. However, he began very humbly in New York.

He was born on July 19, 1953, in Brooklyn, New York, and grew up poor in the Canarsie Bayview housing projects. To escape the thoughts of being poor, he turned to sports and became an outstanding basketball player in high school.

Schultz received an athletic scholarship to Northern Michigan University, becoming the first person in his family to attend college. After graduating with a degree in business and marketing, he worked at a variety of jobs until he landed a job as a salesperson for Xerox Corporation. This enabled him to stabilize his young career and develop his strong work ethic.

In 1979, he took a position that proved to be a blessing in disguise—general manager for the Swedish drip coffee maker manufacturer, Hammarplast. This first step onto a yellow brick road was the defining point in his life; this career move would present three opportunities that would shape his professional future.

Schultz's winding road began to straighten out in 1981. His first opportunity came as a result of his love for coffee and his Industrious Nature, which led him to travel to Seattle and check out a Hammarplast customer, a popular coffee bean store chain called Starbucks. A year later the owners invited Schultz to join them as their director of marketing.

The second opportunity came when, while on a business trip to Milan, Italy, Schultz noted that coffee bars existed on practically every street and they served excellent espresso. These bars also served as meeting places for small groups, which he viewed as social networking. These observations sparked a concept that would eventually take the world by storm.

He described what he thought was a brilliant model, the café concept, to the owners of Starbucks, suggesting that in addition to their whole bean coffee, leaf teas and spices, they should offer traditional espresso beverages. After a successful pilot of the café concept, the owners refused to roll it out companywide. Their main reason was that they did not want to get into the restaurant or café business.

Frustrated, but not defeated, Schultz refused to let his dream die. He started his own coffee shop named Il Giornale in 1985. Two years later, the third opportunity knocked when the original Starbucks management decided to focus on Peet's Coffee & Tea and sold its Starbucks retail unit to Schultz and Il Giornale for $3.8 million.

Immediately after acquiring Starbucks, Schultz changed Il Giornale's name to Starbucks and aggressively expanded Starbucks' reach across the United States. This bold step placed Schultz among the top entrepreneurs in the world. Soon Starbucks was in nearly every city in America and every country in the world.

With success comes a degree of independence, and Schultz exercised his. He did not believe in franchising, so he made a point of having Starbucks own every domestic outlet with one exception. According to Wikipedia, he went 50-50 with Magic Johnson on stores in minority communities.

In 2008, Schultz earned a total compensation of nearly $10 million. While earning money was not his primary dream, his income was a comfortable and well received by-product.

Schultz is an excellent example of how you should take advantage of opportunities. They present themselves to you even though other people may disagree with you and your vision or dream. You must trust your gut feeling, instinct, and insight. Understanding is key; no one may see your vision as clearly as you. Therefore, you may have to step onto the yellow brick road all by yourself.

It is all about trusting in what the Creator has placed in you. Your Industrious Nature will bring your dream into reality under the condition that you trust the dream.

Sometimes your dream may not come to you as a result of your work or employment, as in the case of Howard Schultz. It may be a vision that you have had since childhood, or it could be a dream that just stays with you as in the case of Phil Knight.

Philip Hampson Knight had a vision of an athletic shoe company while he was still a student at the Stanford Graduate School of Business. Today, Knight is known as the co-founder and chairman of the largest athletic shoe company in the world, Nike. He resigned as the company's chief executive officer in 2004, while retaining the position of chairman of the board. As of 2007, Knight was the 30th richest American.

Unlike Howard Schultz, Knight did not grow up poor. He was born February 24, 1938, in Portland, Oregon, the son of a lawyer and future newspaper publisher. While not the son of a billionaire, he was afforded the lifestyle of a wealthy family. Although several excellent choices of endeavors were available to him, Knight graduated from the University of Oregon in 1959 with a degree in journalism, most likely to prepare for a career in publishing.

Knight's dream came as result of his interest in track, which he ran as a middle-distance runner at the University of Oregon under track coach Bill Bowerman.

Right after graduating from Oregon, Knight enlisted in the Army. He served a year of active duty, and then spent some time in the Army Reserves. While still in the Army Reserves, he enrolled at the Stanford Graduate School of Business, where the seed of entrepreneurial spirit took hold during Frank Shallenberger's small business class. In a *Stanford Magazine* article, Knight recalled, "That class was an 'aha' moment....Shallenberger defined the type of person who was an entrepreneur—and I realized he was talking to me. I remember saying to myself: 'this is really what I would like to do'." Once Knight focused, his Industrious Nature automatically began functioning intently in the area of his single-most-important-interest.

Knight created a business plan based on his paper, *"Can Japanese Sports Shoes Do to German Sports Shoes What Japanese Cameras Did to German Cameras?"* The question became his armor and fueled his Industrious Nature to focus on selling running shoes.

Ironically, Knight's career had been somewhat planned by virtue of the success of his father and family. Most people accept a future that promises security and comfort such as the one that was readied for Knight. However, deep in his soul was an entrepreneur seeking to come into reality.

Armed with a master's degree in business administration in 1962, Knight took a trip to see the world. One of his stops was in Kobe, Japan. Kobe was the city in which the Tiger brand running shoe was manufactured by Onitsuka, Co. Impressed with the quality and low cost of this running shoe, Knight was determined to meet with the owner of the company. Without any formal introduction, he called Onitsuka, who agreed to meet with him.

As the result of trusting his gut feeling, by the end of the meeting, Knight had secured distribution rights for the western United States to sell the Tiger brand running shoes.

He returned to Portland, Oregon, with a deal that promised only an opportunity and the freedom to exercise it. With this chance, however small it seemed at first, he ordered his first Tiger samples, which took more than a year to be shipped to him. By this time, he had become employed as an accountant in Portland. However, as soon as he received the shoe samples, he began his marketing plan.

He mailed two pairs to his old track coach, Bill Bowerman, who was well known as a brilliant coach for the University of Oregon. His specialty was training long distance runners, some of whom were of Olympic caliber, such as Steve PreFontaine who attended the University when Knight did.

To help PreFontaine take better advantage of his running style, Coach Bowerman designed a special running shoe for him. The shoe was lightweight with a unique sole that looked like the grid on an old style waffle iron. In fact, several stories indicated that the coach got the idea from the waffle iron his wife used to make breakfast. The unique running shoe proved to be very efficient.

When the coach received the Tiger running shoe from Knight, he was not only interested in purchasing and endorsing it, but he also informed Knight that he would like to become a partner and provide design ideas for better running shoes. The two men shook hands on a partnership on January 25, 1964, the birth date of Blue Ribbon Sports, forerunner to Nike.

Determined to make his dream a reality, for five years, 26-year-old Knight peddled Onitsuka running shoes from the back of his green Plymouth Valiant at track meets across the Pacific Northwest. He continued this process until he was able to leave his accountant job and work full time for Blue Ribbon Sports.

The next step on the road to success was the development and procurement of the powerful Nike logo. Carolyn Davidson, a member of Knight's team, suggested that the company use Nike, the name of a Greek goddess, as its name instead of Blue Ribbon Sports. Although Knight did not take to the name, he and the team agreed to go with it. The famous Swoosh logo was not far behind.

The stage was now set for Knight to turn a tiny company into the world's largest athletic shoe and apparel company. Today Nike Corp. is a multibillion-dollar enterprise and a household name.

Knight had faith and trusted his insight; his single-most-important-interest guided him from one achievement to the next. He also had confidence in suggestions or opinions of those who worked with him. This is especially true in the one incident that established Nike as a cultural icon.

Sports was the glue that bonded Knight's idea to its practical application. He harnessed society's adoration of heroes and its passion for status symbols with a marketing plan that focused on tying the product to an athlete with a singularly charismatic sports image.

In 1984, the company signed a 21-year-old basketball player out of the University of North Carolina who was headed for the National Basketball Association, but had not yet played professionally. Again, Knight's gut feelings and insight paid off because the youngster Nike signed to endorse its unique basketball sneaker was Michael Jordan, soon be known to the world as Air Jordan.

As Jordan soared though the air on basketball courts and into the hearts and minds of the youth, Nike soared to the top of the apparel industry, dwarfing its competitors. Within a year, nearly everyone wanted to be "like Mike," and nearly every American boy was wearing Nike's Air Jordan high-top sneakers as a status symbol. Knight said, "It wasn't planning. We could see that he [Jordan] was a charismatic guy who jumps over the moon and is very competitive, but nobody could have predicted what he would become to our culture."

Although Knight's goal did not focus on money, the accumulation of wealth was a wonderful by-product that has enabled him to aid others. He has contributed millions of dollars to the University of Oregon, the Cancer Institute at Oregon Health & Science University, the Stanford Graduate School of Business, and his high school alma mater.

What started as a dream in the mind of Knight while he was back in graduate school ended as a magnificent example of the power of the Industrious Nature locked in all of us just waiting to be unleashed.

You, like Phil Knight, must trust your feelings and be true to your dream. He did not know what the outcome would be, but he trusted that the opportunity was dependent upon his Will and desire. Just remember that the darkness comes before the light, and count on the knowledge that daybreak is on the way.

Schultz focused on his love of coffee and devising new and better ways to market what he loved. Knight convinced himself and a few friends that he could tap into the athletic shoe market. At the age of 76, Grandma Moses, a self-taught artist, became an integral part of art history. Each person's success is a testimony for every human being.

Note also that Schultz and Knight had business degrees, demonstrating how education can increase your chances of success.

However, despite all the factors Moses, Schultz and Knight had in common, none had to contend with the same type of obstacles Oprah Winfrey faced.

According to some assessments, Oprah Winfrey is the most influential woman in the world. The billionaire media mogul is best known for her self-titled, multi-award winning talk show, *The Oprah Winfrey Show*, produced by her own company and the highest-rated program of its kind in history.

Interestingly, she had less of a chance to achieve this tremendous status than most of you. Her rise is not just about circumstances, it is sponsored by what comes from within. What drove her to succeed is not unique or exclusively hers—it is also within you. In fact, your beginning may had been much better than hers.

Oprah Gail Winfrey was born January 29, 1954, into poverty in rural Kosciusko, Mississippi, to an unwed teenage mother and a father who was in the Armed Forces at the time of her birth. Her mother, Vernita Lee, was a housemaid, and her father, Vernon

Winfrey, was a coal miner who later worked as a barber before becoming a city councilman.

After giving birth, Winfrey's mother traveled north, leaving Winfrey to spend her first six years living with her grandmother, Hattie Mae Lee, who was so poor that Winfrey often wore dresses made of potato sacks, which led to teasing by the local children.

Her grandmother taught her to read before the age of three and took her to the local church, where she was nicknamed "The Preacher" for her ability to recite Bible verses. When Winfrey was a child, her grandmother would take a switch and hit her with it when she didn't do her chores or if she misbehaved in any way.

At age six, Winfrey moved to an inner-city neighborhood in Milwaukee, Wisconsin, with her mother, who worked long hours as a maid and could not spend much time with her young daughter.

Winfrey has stated that she was molested by her cousin, her uncle, and a family friend, starting when she was nine years old, something she first revealed to her viewers on a 1986 episode of her TV show dealing with the topic of sexual abuse.

Despite her home life, Oprah managed to do well in school, skipping two of her earliest grades. She received a scholarship to attend Nicolet High School in the Milwaukee suburb of Glendale, Wisconsin. However, the bitter reality of her abuse compelled her to run away from home.

She became pregnant at age 14, but her son died shortly after birth. Her frustrated mother sent her to live with her father, Vernon, in Nashville, Tennessee.

Her father was strict and made Winfrey's education a priority. In high school, she was an honor student and received many awards. She attracted the attention of the local Black radio station, WVOL, which hired her part-time to do the local news. She continued to work for the station during her college years at Tennessee State University.

Shortly after, Winfrey began working as the first Black female and youngest news anchor at Nashville's

WLAC-TV. From this point, her life in the media began taking shape.

She moved to Baltimore's WJZ-TV in 1976 to co-anchor the six o'clock news. Soon afterwards, she joined Richard Sher as co-host of WJZ's local talk show, *People Are Talking.* She also hosted the local version of *Dialing for Dollars.*

By 1983, Oprah relocated to Chicago to host WLS-TV's low-rated half-hour morning talk show, *AM Chicago.* This was a defining moment of opportunity in her career.

Her first episode aired on January 2, 1984. Within months, the show went from last place in the ratings to overtaking *Donahue* as the highest rated talk show in Chicago. It was renamed *The Oprah Winfrey Show,* expanded to a full hour, and syndicated nationally. It became the number one day-time talk show in America.

Time magazine wrote, "Few people would have bet on Oprah Winfrey's swift rise to host of the most popular talk show on TV."

However, one person who would have bet on her was her grandmother, who was not surprised about Winfrey's career choice. She recalled that ever since Oprah could talk, she was "on stage," playing games interviewing her corncob doll and the crows on the fence of her family's property. Winfrey later acknowledged her grandmother's influence, saying it was Hattie Mae who had encouraged her to speak in public and "gave me a positive sense of myself."

As an American television host, producer, and philanthropist, Winfrey, along with Harold Schultz and Phil Knight, is ranked as one of the richest Americans of the 21st century. They realized that you can not sit and wait for opportunity to knock; if you do, you will have a long wait and receive nothing in the end.

They knew that you must challenge your idea by working to develop it. You will find that opportunity will open just like an oyster opens to give up its beautiful pearl. Like thousands before her, Winfrey reached inside, focused, and allowed her interest to fuel her Industrious Nature to achieve her dream. She battled life and faced her challenges with consistent progress.

On the broad stage of life, some achievers are up against what seem to be insurmountable odds. The circumstance can be so overwhelming that for the person to just take a breath of fresh air would be a victory. That was the predicament Melody Gardot faced.

Singer and songwriter Melody Gardot confronted a physical challenge, an accident that left her with no physical mobility or verbal skills and a severely damaged memory. The most optimistic analysis was that she was fortunate be alive.

Born February 2, 1985, in New Jersey, Gardot was a normal child in every way. She was raised for the most part by her grandparents because her mother was a photographer whose work kept her on the road.

Gardot developed a deep interest in music and started taking music lessons at the age of nine. The piano was her favorite instrument. By the time she was sixteen, she was playing in Philadelphia bars on Friday and

Saturday nights. Her musical tastes ranged from The Mamas & the Papas to Duke Ellington, and she was greatly influenced by such blues and jazz artists as Judy Garland, Janis Joplin, and Miles Davis. She also appreciated George Gershwin and Latin musical greats such as Stan Getz and Caetano Veloso.

While cycling in Philadelphia in November 2003, Gardot was struck by a Jeep Cherokee whose driver had run a red light. She suffered serious head and spinal injuries and her pelvis was shattered in two places. She was confined to her hospital bed for a year.

The neural pathways between her brain's two cortexes, which control perception and higher mental function, were badly damaged, making communication nearly impossible as she struggled to recall the right words to express her thoughts and feelings. Additionally, she was left hyper-sensitive to both light and sound and wore sunglasses at nearly all times.

To make matters worse, she also suffered long- and short-term memory loss and had difficulty with her sense of time. Gardot has likened waking each day with no memory to "climbing Mount Everest every day."

After her release from the hospital, she traveled with a physiotherapist and wore a TENS machine strapped to her waist which released pain reducing impulses.

Thanks to her Industrious Nature, her recovery began making real progress. She began to experiment with macrobiotics, which helped her to relax mentally and cope with her pain. She cooked for several hours a day, a routine that helped take her mind off her physical condition and sleep more easily.

However, the real turning point came when she began to focus on her single-most-important-interest, music. Her Industrious Nature swung into high gear and found new ways for her to express her interest. She began writing music, and learned how to play the guitar and hum. Listening to music and making a verbal attempt to sing or hum helped her brain to form new neural pathways. This is proof that the brain and the body, as part of the Industrious Nature, function together to achieve your goal. Through music, Gardot regained her brain function, improved her speech, and lifted her spirits.

Soon she was singing again and writing original songs. The rest seemed to come easily. She assembled a demo which was picked up by Universal Records. Subsequently, her first full length album, *Worrisome Heart*, was released in 2008. After meeting her in New York City in 2008, producer Larry Klein began working with Gardot and they released her second album, *My One and Only Thrill*, on April 28, 2009.

Gardot is a living testimony to the power of the Industrious Nature that is in all of us. We can see in her that the Industrious Nature can redirect and find a pathway to success as a result of our single-most-important-interest. It cannot be said enough, "From hard work and perseverance comes opportunity after opportunity."

Gardot, unlike many other achievers, had to overcome tremendous physical challenges that came in adulthood—which did not make her tasks any easier. However, on some occasions, a physical challenge can occur at birth or in childhood, which can make achievement seem even more difficult. That is what happened with Ray Charles Robinson.

Ray Charles Robinson was born September 23, 1930, in Albany, Georgia, to Aretha Williams, a sharecropper, and Bailey Robinson, a railroad repair man, mechanic and handyman. When Robinson was an infant, the family moved to the poor Black community of Jellyroll on the western side of Greenville, Florida. When he was five years old, Robinson witnessed the death of his younger brother, George. By the time he was seven, he was totally blind.

Like Gardot, Robinson showed an early interest in music and received his first piano lesson from Wiley Pit, a stride pianist who played boogie woogie at his club, Pit's Red Wing Café.

Robinson's mother taught him to use his memory and hearing as tools to find his way, and then sent him to the Florida School for the Deaf and the Blind in St. Augustine, Florida. During his nearly ten years there, Robinson developed his interest in music, and learned to read and write in Braille. He studied classical music, but never lost his fascination with the pulsing rhythms of gospel, rhythm and blues and other popular genres.

While at school, he played with the Adderley brothers, Nat and Cannonball, and began playing gigs with Lawyer Smith and his Band in 1943 at the Red Bird Club and DeLuxe Club in Frenchtown and roadhouses around Tallahassee, as well as the Governor's Ball. He learned to arrange music, sing like Nat King Cole and other heroes, and soon became the premiere musician at the school.

When his mother died, Robinson did not return to school, but continued pursuing his single-most-important-interest, music. His dream was to have a band of his own, so he moved across the country to Seattle in 1947 to start fresh. As part of the McSons Trio, he recorded his first hit, *Confession Blues,* for the Down Beat label in 1949. The song soared to #2 on the R&B charts. Then, he joined Swing Time Records and began using the name "Ray Charles" to avoid being confused with the very popular boxer, Sugar Ray Robinson.

When Swing Time ran into financial difficulty, they sold his contract to Atlantic Records, where his *I Got a Woman* brought him to national prominence.

After releasing a series of chart-topping hits, Charles left Atlantic for a more lucrative deal with ABC-Paramount Records (later renamed ABC Records) in 1960. With this move, he demonstrated his skill as a businessman and entrepreneur by engineering, with the help of the Shaw Agency, a deal which was nearly unheard of in the industry. He got a higher royalty rate, complete artistic control and eventual ownership of the master tapes.

More chart-toppers such as *Georgia On My Mind, Hit the Road Jack, Unchain My Heart,* and *I Can't Stop Loving You,* cemented his success in nearly every musical category, including Rhythm and Blues, Soul, Rock and Roll, Blues, Jazz, Country, and Pop. In 1963, Charles founded his own record label, Tangerine Records, which ABC-Paramount distributed.

Despite his success as a musical artist, he faced another challenge—an addiction to heroin that nearly destroyed him, his family and his career. He had become addicted to the drug in the early 50's when he was about 20 years old. Like many young people without parental guidance, some of the decisions he made were bad.

In 1965, Charles was arrested for possession for the third time. Faced with jail and the loss of his family and career, he made the decision to kick the habit. He entered a clinic in Los Angeles, and with the Will that the Creator gave him, kicked the addiction "cold turkey." He never touched heroin again.

Over the next 40 years, Charles continued to produce hit records, win Grammy Awards and sell out concerts, becoming one of the world's most beloved entertainers. As celebrated as he became, he never forgot his roots and contributed more than $20 million to African-American colleges and charities for the blind and deaf.

In 2004, *Rolling Stone* ranked Charles number 10 on its list of "The 100 Greatest Artists of All Time," and voted him number two on its November 2008 list of "The 100 Greatest Singers of All Time."

Out of total darkness, this musical icon created a never ending light in the world with sound. He used sound to understand the world outside and to express his world inside.

Ray's history is not much different from that of other successful achievers of his time and those who came before him. What made Charles different was that he used his Industrious Nature to overcome both a physical disability and a serious addiction to achieve his dream.

None of these achievers, especially Grandma Moses, who started her career at age 78, was imprisoned by time. They focused on their single-most-important-interest as their life's goal. Their Industrious Nature functioned automatically to bring the dream into reality, no matter how immense the challenges seemed to be to others.

The life stories of these achievers were obtained from the Wikipedia free encyclopedia online. There are many sources you can use to examine the interests that fire up the Industrious Nature of achievers in all walks of life and in every endeavor. If you can't go online, then go to the public library, where you can study the lives of successful achievers.

These are not stories about great people; these are stories about ordinary people who became great. As you study them, you will find that they are very similar in one very important aspect: their Industrious Nature is driven by their single-most-important-interest. While they don't all have the same exact interests, they used their insight, education, skills and good work ethic to take advantage of every opportunity that appeared, in order to achieve their specific dreams.

They overcame their fears and inhibitions, and they wasted little or no time on failure; their energy and efforts were and are focused on achieving a goal.

The one thing you must remember is that just as they were, you were created to be successful. Your Industrious Nature will obey your Will regardless of your age, race, sex, economic status or beginning in life. You have only to believe it and it will automatically function. To achieve your dreams, unleash the power of your Industrious Nature and success is automatic. You are the only one you must convince.

The Beginning....

About the Author

Shahid Abdullah, who has degrees in art and sociology, began his career as a fashion designer in 1968, but put his artistic aspirations on hold to become a financial planner. He gradually returned to his designing and, by the fall of 1998, had perfected the concept and look of his *Bilalian®* styles, a line of suits, shirts and ensembles that represent a cultural revolution in men's fashion for a new generation of men.

A member of the Muslim Community since 1968, Abdullah is the Imam of the Masjid Al-Hadi in Elizabeth, N.J. He is the proud son of Elige and Alice Souels, and the father of four adult children, Ahmed, Jamillah, Fatimah and Rabih Abdullah. He has one grandchild, Khadijah Barr.

Abdullah resides in New Jersey, where he operates his fashion company, The New Breed Generation, Inc. *Success is Automatic* is his first book. His second book, *The Spirit of Bilal: A Community Is Born, will soon be published*, and he is working on his next book, *The River of Gold.*

For more information, visit www.thegoldentree.com. To share your comments on Success is Automatic *or to order other books, write to:*

Shahid Abdullah at PO Box 332, Roselle, NJ 07203

or e-mail him at: *shahid_abdullah2000@yahoo.com.*

Use this page to begin your journey to success.

MY SINGLE-MOST-IMPORTANT-INTEREST IS: